CAMBRIDGE

Big Book Stories

Four Rabbits

Sam and Nico are at school.

'Come in. Put your bag on your peg,'
says the teacher. *'Let's count 1, 2, 3!'*
'1, 2, 3!' count the class.
'Well done! I'm happy!'
'Where's Rabbit?' says Greenman.

'Let's count the circles!' says the teacher.
'1, 2, 3!' count the class.
'Let's count the squares!'
'1, 2, 3!'
'Let's count the triangles!'
'1, 2, 3!'
'Let's count the rectangles!'
'1, 2, 3!'
'Well done! You are good!'

'Let's count the rabbits!' says the teacher.

'1, 2, 3... 4!'

'Four...? There are three rabbits. There aren't four.'

'Oh, it's Rabbit!' says Sam.

'Oh, no! It's Rabbit!' says Greenman.

'There are 1, 2, 3 rabbits,' says the teacher. *'There aren't four!'*

'Rabbit, come here!' says Greenman.

'Let's count the rabbits!' says the teacher.

'1, 2, 3... 4! On the chair!'

'Oh...! There are four rabbits! Naughty rabbit!'

'This is Stella, Frog and Hedgehog.
And this is Greenman!' says Nico.

'We are friends!' says Sam.

'Hello!' says the class.

'I'm sorry!' says Rabbit.

The Honey Game

Sam, Nico and Greenman are in the forest.

'Greenman! Let's play on the swing!' says Sam.
'Greenman! Let's play on the seesaw!' says Frog.
'Greenman! Let's play in the sandpit!' says Nico.
'Greenman! Let's play on the slide!' says Stella.
'No, thanks,' says Greenman.

'Oh, no! There's no honey!'

'Hello, Greenman. Let's play!' says Frog.

'Hello, Frog. No, thanks. Yummy, there's honey!'

'Let's follow the honey up, up, up the tree,' says Frog. *'Let's use the seesaw.'*

'Good idea!'

'Jump up and down like me!'

'I'm up the tree! I'm so happy! I like the seesaw! Now, where's my honey?'

'Hello, Greenman. Let's play!'
says Stella.

*'Hello, snake. No, thanks.
Yummy, there's honey!'*

*'Let's follow the honey down,
down, down the tree,'* says
Stella. *'Let's use the slide.'*

'Good idea!'

'Slide down like me,' says Stella.

'I'm down the tree! I'm so happy. I like the slide. Now, where's my honey?'

'Here's your honey!' say Sam and Nico.

'Thank you! I like honey. And I like the seesaw and the slide!'

'Yay! Let's play!' says Sam.

'Let's play!' says Greenman.

I'm Hurt!

Sam, Nico and Greenman are going for a walk in the forest. It's a windy day. They are very happy.

'I like the forest. I go up and down!' says Sam.

'I like the forest. I go up and down!' says Nico.

'Up, down! Up, down!'

'It's a windy day. Remember, be careful!' says Greenman.

'Be careful!' says Greenman.
'Oh, no! I'm hurt!' says Nico.
'I can help!'
'My leg! My foot!'

'Be careful!' says Greenman.
'Oh, no! I'm hurt,' says Sam.
'I can help!'
'My hand! My finger!'

'What's the matter, Nico?' says Greenman.

'My leg hurts.'

'Can you move your leg?'

'Yes, I can.'

'Good! But your leg is dirty. Let's clean it and put on a plaster.'

'I've got a plaster!' says Sam.

'What's the matter,
Sam?' says
Greenman.

'My hand hurts.
My finger hurts.'

'Can you move your
fingers?'

'Yes, I can.'

'1, 2, 3, 4… Four
fingers! Oh, no!
You are hurt!'
says Greenman.

'No!' says Nico. *'1, 2, 3, 4, 5!*
Five fingers! Your finger is dirty!'
'Let's clean it and put on a plaster,'
says Greenman.

'Remember, be careful!'

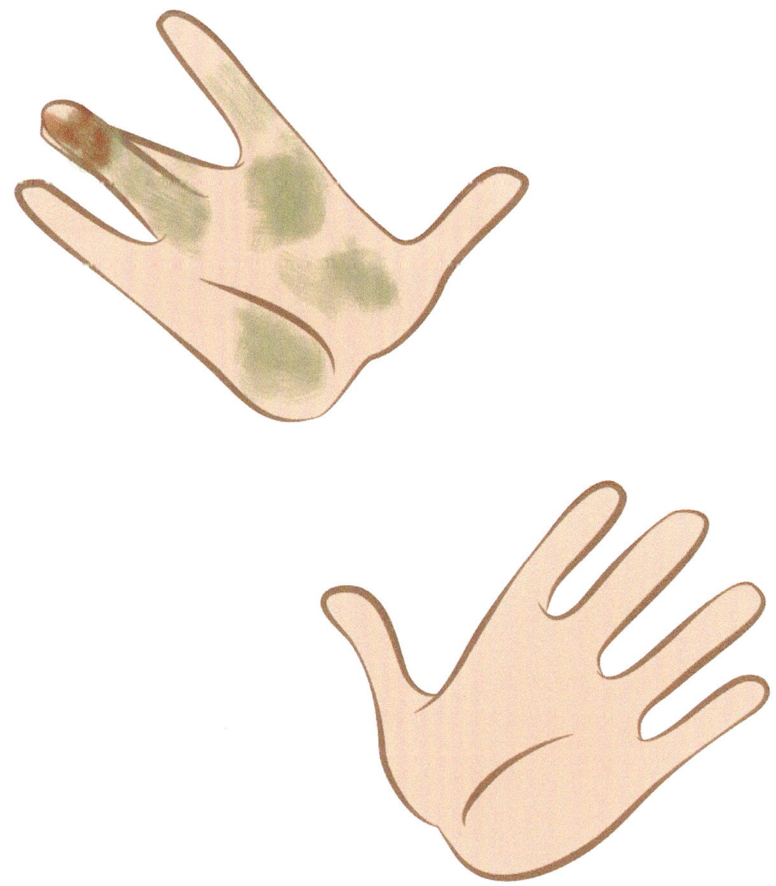

It's Too Small!

It's winter time. It's windy. Sam and Nico are cold. Rabbit is sad.

'Hello, Rabbit. What's the matter?' says Greenman.

'Hello, Greenman. I'm hungry!' says Rabbit.

'Where are your carrots?'

'I haven't got any carrots. Look, the birds are eating them!'

'Oh, no!' says Greenman.

'Oh, no! My hat! I'm cold!' says Sam.

'I'm cold. Let's go home!' says Nico.

'Let's put on winter clothes!' says Sam.

'Good idea!' says Nico.

Sam is at home. She's putting on her winter clothes.

'Sam, you can't wear your pink dress,' says Mum. *'You can't wear your purple boots.'*

'I like my pink dress!' says Sam. *'I like my purple boots!'*

'Your dress is too small. Your boots are too small. Please, take them off!'

Nico is at home. He's putting on his winter clothes.

'Nico, you can't wear your winter jumper,' says Dad. *'You can't wear your winter trousers.'*

'I like my winter jumper!' says Nico. *'I like my winter trousers!'*

'Your jumper is too small. Your trousers are too small. Please, take them off!'

'You can't put the clothes in the bin!' says Sam.

'But I can't wear the jumper. I can't wear the trousers!' says Nico.

'What can we do with them?'

'Greenman!' say Sam and Nico.

'Look!' says Nico. *'Greenman is wearing your purple boots, my winter jumper and my winter trousers!'*

'He's a scarecrow. The birds are scared!' says Sam.

'Rabbit has got carrots to eat.'

'And we are recycling the clothes!'

'Boo!' says Greenman.

Can I Help You?

Hedgehog is in the forest.

'I'm sad. Where are my friends? says Hedgehog. *'There's the farm. I can see my friends!'*

'Hello, Bird,' says
Hedgehog.

'Hello, Hedgehog,'
says Bird.

'Can I help you?'

'Can you fly?'

'No, I can't.'

'Have you got
strong wings?'

'No, I haven't.'

'I'm sorry. You can't
help me.'

'OK. Bye bye!'

'Hello, Horse,' says Hedgehog.

'Hello, Hedgehog,' says Horse.

'Can I help you?'

'Can you run?'

'No, I can't.'

'Have you got strong legs?'

'No, I haven't.'

'I'm sorry. You can't help me.'

'OK. Bye bye!'

'Hello, Rabbit. It's smelly!' says Hedgehog.

'Hello, Hedgehog,' says Rabbit.

'Can I help you?'

'Can you jump?'

'No, I can't.'

'Have you got strong arms?'

'No, I haven't.'

'I'm sorry. You can't help me.'

'OK. Bye bye!'

'Hello, Greenman.'

'Hello, Hedgehog. What's the matter?'

'I can't help Bird, Horse or Rabbit. I can't fly, run or jump.'

'But you are strong! You are special! You have got strong spikes!'

'I am strong! I can help!' says Hedgehog.
'Well done, Hedgehog!' says Greenman.
'Thank you, Hedgehog!' says Rabbit.

SUMMER PARTY!

The Summer Party

Sam, Nico and Greenman are in the forest.

'Hello, Sam. Hello, Nico. What are you doing?' says Greenman.

'We're having a summer party,' says Nico.

'And what's the matter?'

'Fox has got the food!' says Sam

'Oh, no!'

'I'm hungry and thirsty,' says Nico.

'I'm hungry and thirsty too,' says Sam.

'I've got an idea!' says Greenman.

'Yummy!' says Fox.
'Food for me!'

'Hello, Greenman,' says Hen.

'Hello, Hen. Have you got any eggs?'

'Yes, I have.'

'Can I have some eggs, please?'

'Yes. I like sharing my eggs. Here you are.'

'Thank you!'

'1, 2, 3, 4, 5, 6.'

'Hello, Greenman,' says Rabbit.

'Hello, Rabbit. Have you got any carrots?'

'Yes, I have.'

'Can I have some carrots, please?'

'Yes. I like sharing my carrots. Here you are.'

'Thank you!'

'1, 2, 3, 4, 5, 6.'

'Hello Greenman,' says Tree.

'Hello Tree. Have you got any plums?'

'Yes, I have.'

'Can I have some plums, please?'

'Yes. I like sharing my plums. Here you are.'

'Thank you!'

'1, 2, 3, 4, 5, 6.'

'Hello, Fox.'

'Hello, Greenman. I'm sorry. I'm sad on my own. Can I share my food too?'

'Yes. We like sharing. Here you are.'

SUMMER PARTY!

'Welcome to the summer party!' says Sam.

'Thank you for the food,' says Nico.

'I like sharing my eggs,' says Hen.

'I like sharing my carrots,' says Rabbit.

'I like sharing my plums,' says Tree.

'I like sharing my food too,' says Fox.

'I'm hungry and thirsty. Let's eat! Happy summer, everyone!' says Greenman.

Unit 1 *Four Rabbits*

Unit 2 *The Honey Game*

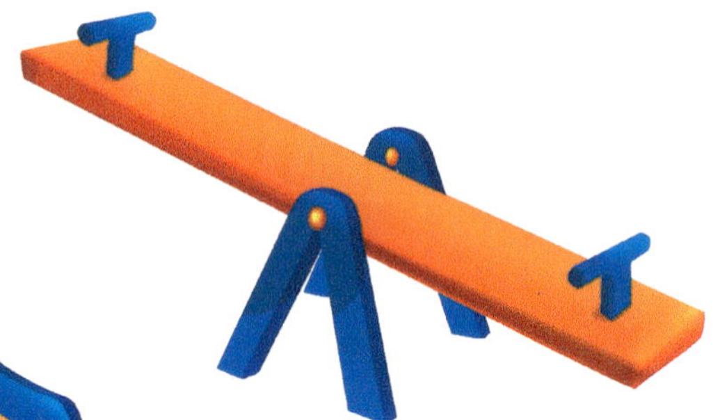

Unit 3 *I'm Hurt!*

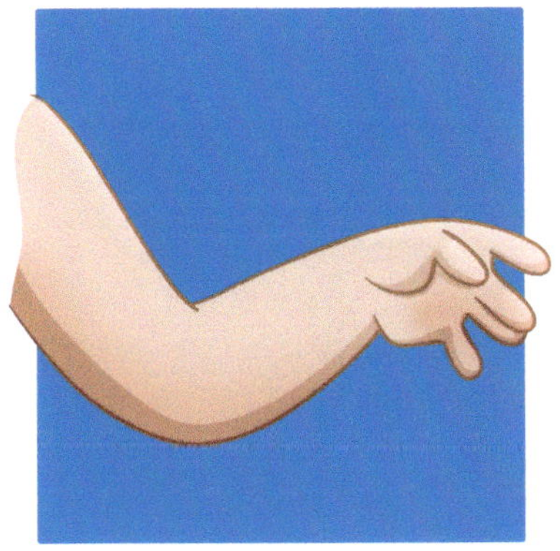
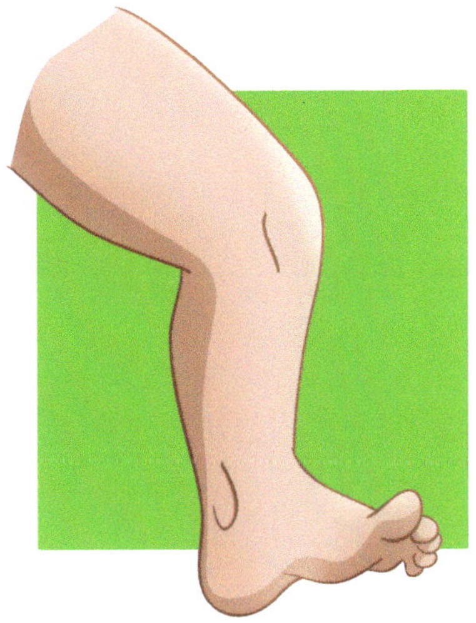
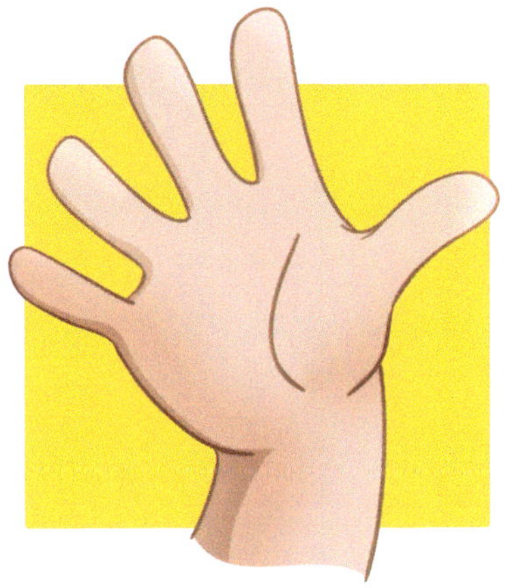
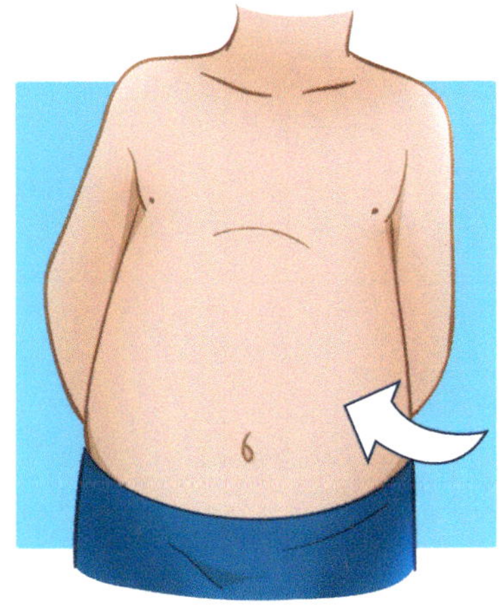
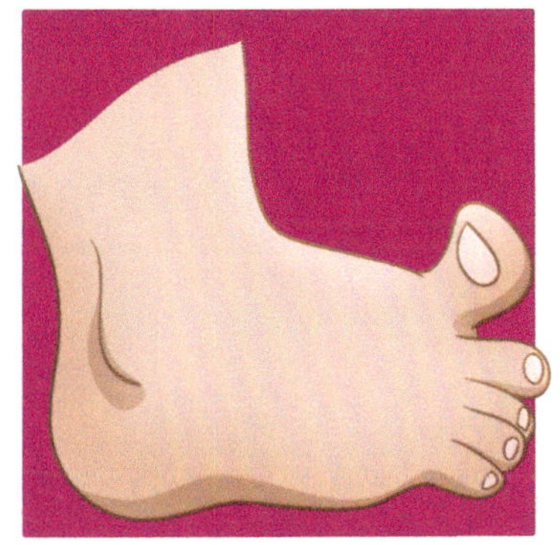
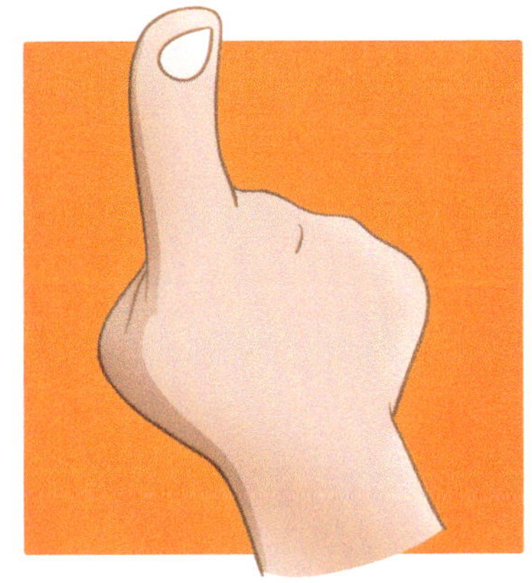

Unit 4 *It's Too Small!*

Unit 5 *Can I Help You?*

Unit 6 *The Summer Party*

Goodbye!

CAMBRIDGE
UNIVERSITY PRESS

University Printing House, Cambridge CB2 8BS, United Kingdom

One Liberty Plaza, 20th Floor, New York, NY 10006, USA

477 Williamstown Road, Port Melbourne, VIC 3207, Australia

314–321, 3rd Floor, Plot 3, Splendor Forum, Jasola District Centre, New Delhi – 110025, India

103 Penang Road, #05-06/07, Visioncrest Commercial, Singapore 238467

José Abascal 56, 1° – 28003 Madrid, Spain

Cambridge University Press is part of the University of Cambridge.
It furthers the University's mission by disseminating knowledge in the pursuit of education, learning and research at the highest international levels of excellence.

www.cambridge.org

First published 2015

20 19 18 17 16 15 14 13

Printed in Spain by Pulmen
Legal deposit: M-3618-2015

ISBN 978-8-490-36826-8 Big Book A
ISBN 978-8-490-36825-1 Pupil's Book A (with Stickers and Pop-outs)
ISBN 978-8-490-36827-5 Teacher's Book A
ISBN 978-8-490-36828-2 Guía Didáctica A
ISBN 978-8-490-36829-9 Teacher's Resource Book A
ISBN 978-8-490-36831-2 Flashcards A
ISBN 978-8-490-36830-5 Phonics Flashcards A
ISBN 978-8-490-36832-9 Class Audio CDs A
ISBN 978-8-490-36833-6 Digital Forest A
ISBN 978-8-490-36845-9 Routine Board
ISBN 978-8-490-36000-2 Reward Stickers
ISBN 978-8-490-36001-9 Reward Stamp
ISBN 978-8-490-36846-6 Teacher's Bag
ISBN 978-8-490-36844-2 Puppet

Thanks and Acknowledgements

Author's thanks
Many thanks to everyone at Cambridge University Press. In particular, to Jeannine Bogaard and Julieta Hernández for providing the opportunity to write, and to Mercedes López de Bergara for her continued support.
A special thank you goes to Juan González Cué, our Production Project Manager.

We would also like to thank all the teachers for their help in reviewing the material and for the invaluable feedback they provided:
Álvaro Ruiz González, Colegio Ramón y Cajal, Madrid; Carlos B. Ferrer de las Peñas, Colegio Montpellier, Madrid; Paloma del Cerro Gómez, CEIPSO El Greco, Madrid; Miriam Martínez de Dios, Colegio La Anunciata, Madrid; María Palomo Bosque, Colegio San José, Madrid; Carmen García, Salesianos Atocha, Madrid; Gloria Torrecilla González, Colegio El Valle, Madrid; Cristina Álvarez, Colegio Ramón Gómez de la Serna, Madrid; Mª Jesús Aragón Rodríguez, CEIP Velázquez, Madrid; Leyre Alcalde Gordo, CEIP La Alameda, Madrid; Mª Cruz Salomon García, CEIP Infanta Leonor, Madrid; José Rubén Jiménez Carvajal, CEIP Seseña y Benavente, Madrid; Antonio Hernández García, Colegio Santa Joaquina de Vedruna de Sevilla, Sevilla; Sara Fernández Moratilla, Colegio Virgen del Carmen, Barcelona; Raúl Vercher Gómez, Colegio Sagrada Familia, Valencia; Joaquín Martínez Rueda, Colegio Narval, Murcia; Silvia Crespo Rica, Colegio Santo Tomás de Villanueva, Granada; Vanesa Rubio Carreño, CEIP La Pea, Valencia; Lidia Madroñal Vaquero, Colegio Santa Joaquina de Vedruna, Sevilla; María Del Mar Jiménez Calvillo, CEIP Las Cigüeñas, Madrid; María José Cortés Moreno, CEIP La Raza, Sevilla; Rosa Mª Montané Milà, ZER Cep de Sis, Barcelona; Raquel Lara Sánchez, Colegio La Milagrosa, Madrid; María José Pascual Núñez, CEIP Monte Alegre, Valencia; Inmaculada Folgado Aliaga, Colegio Asunción de Nuestra Señora, Valencia.

The authors and publishers are grateful to the following illustrators:
Gema García Ingelmo: illustration
Alfredo Hernando Torres: additional illustration

The publishers are grateful to the following contributors:
Teresa del Arco: layout and design
Chefer: cover design